COLOSSAL 24:7

WRITTEN BY
ERIC MICHAEL WESTON

Copyright ©2024,
Eric Michael Weston
ALL RIGHTS RESERVED.

No part of this publication may be reproduced, stored in a retrieval system, or transmitted in any form or by any means—electronic, mechanical, photocopy, recording, or any other—except for brief quotation in reviews, without the prior permission of the author or publisher.

ISBN: 978-1-962402-68-2 (hardcover)
979-83-22418-50-4 (paperback)

Dedication

COLOSSAL 24:7 is for them.

This book is an expansion of my other book, *TRYNA 24:7*.

God is the Regulator; He is the First and Final of all that is in its parking. Christian, Islamist, Hindu, Buddhist, Heathen, these persons are made in His outline, His image. In spite of you not adhering, never coming to faith, God is the vitality of your in and out.

— Eric Michael Weston

CONTENTS

Akimor: A King in My Own Right 1

The Concept of Both 5

Built for It 9

You Will Perform 13

Testament 19

Vocal About Jesus 21

Miracle 25

Medicament 29

Haredim 31

Them That Pray 37

Acknowledgments 41

AKIMOR: A KING IN MY OWN RIGHT

To stand atop that highest mount is unnecessary. It's not the heights, it's the soul in the path to those heights. Height is not a relative of haughtiness. Height is correlating to God's altitude.

Therefore, to go the highest in loftiness, I am not to coed the pride. Pride is the direction to annihilation from within. Triumph, is not unto height or even pride. Triumph is the aftermath of the dominance in war or race; be of humble circumstance.

This is the sling to your grandest shot. Humble circumstance, is not shy or weak in demeanor or essence. Humbleness, is the concept of acknowledging that you have skill and all else, but them that are on this terrain, could have more or just as.

COLOSSAL 24:7

This is tacticality, that you don't show yourself and your multiple dexterity and talent to those who have theirs but do not put it to waste to them that have less. This is the initial track, walking nearest to folks who do not have, to have them have.

God is a God of all, and not subject to few or a solo person of conceit. God is a core-God; manifesting deep purpose in thee for you to wield it in a manner of pleasure to someone who will make it known, that you are right, and a prototype of God.

Eric Michael Weston

    Justice, love moreso than all the attributes, alongside boldness, will be the permanent life to carve yourself into a memorial, to people in the context of being the ultimate via your word and deed. Pray to be ready, ready to be that a king in your own right.

THE CONCEPT OF BOTH

To show affection in piety and devotion, to the vessel which is your aid, to her, she is queen. In every position of your lives, the two shall be shield and sword, she shall be a sword for you, you shall be a shield to her, and the other way back to and for one another.

Your blessings to each other will be counted in the realm untold. Your blessings to them that have no blessed aspiration or anything to that acknowledgement, emit God, bless inside and bless outside that one in the way, yes in The Way.

Hard trials will be worn off, the next level will be more than the other. It's the concept of both, this world is made for both. To this man, fight and peace is what your arsenal is, to the woman, fight and peace, this is your left and right arm.

COLOSSAL 24:7

Traction and valiance will be essential. In everything to you and her, let it all come to these.

BUILT FOR IT

In times, in moments, as the factor that attempts you is in the wire (up close to where you have no choice but to defend), plan to unplan. In your last of moments, you troop that war, war it up. In your desperate lengths, that last act to seize victory, make it known, prevail. Imitate God as it says in His text.

When God believes the combative end will be towards the selected side of the fight, as it is your victory, there shall be no hesitant notion in the run to it. Fore, "Great is His faithfulness; His mercies begin afresh each morning. I say to myself:

"The LORD is my inheritance; therefore, I will hope in him!"

— Lamentations 3: 23-24

The Lord is able to trust His man, His woman, and His nobles,

COLOSSAL 24:7

so then don't yield to the thinking and faith of what is unsure, there's no such faith in what is unsure. There is faith in what is Predestined. That predestined mandate will keep itself accomplished.

To keep yourself to the bar of God: avert the intoxication of this era, world, and trend. The journey, the plow, the toil, it will churn out, best is the man and woman taking in these words.

You know that it is on account of *now,* that alters fate, and curbs future apprehension. It's today in this "now," you need not be trapped to fate.

Fate is the opposing boundary to destiny. Destiny and fate faction over your direction.

Don't let fate dominate your prerogative, hell no! Hell is a hoarder, intending to vacuum all it sees.

YOU WILL PERFORM

Tomorrow is foreign to today, and to the matter at hand, the temporal is identical to vanity. Yes to Divine promise, nay to all which conveys itself to be conflicting and unaccommodating.

Make this today in the vicinity of your victory, make tomorrow graphic as today's accolade. Nothing is official, nothing is written in stone or arraigned in star without God's course of action. It's humbleness to keep Him in a routine thoroughfare, which is modus operandi.

Times will show what people are composed of, binds will prepare the enduring class for the mayhem of all mayhem, the final of this world. To go into this combat, this life, it is speaking unto your constitution, "something is coming forth!"

The devil's head is now in this moment looking in our direction, it's only bold, righteous, and power to gaze back. To succumb

COLOSSAL 24:7

---

to the factor of his deception and lie, is yield.

To avert or stop his missiles, are war-skill. To the one unaware of the controversy, it is the war that began this war, that war, the war out of your management.

Live with thine sword set, thine shield over thee. Live to know you may or may not keep on passing into tomorrow and tomorrows.

As the promise is to be, so will thee and thine for remain. Let God be. Let the night be the flight to morning joy, no time in these hours halt the day at any authority.

Put on might and authority over that devil and his evil, "he who reigns within himself, and rules passions, desires, and fears, is more than a king." — John Milton

This mention is for all humanity. It shouldn't be of everlasting command from mere man their position over the others. God, makes you king, and if He wants, He can forward you to the mud.

From height to hay, from the least of man's considered sight, God may put you where the masses join in acknowledgement towards you, and it won't even be

COLOSSAL 24:7

the highest mountain. Vision is the top of manifesting the proper you in the path to progress.

God is all for man's proportion as well as being. It is the method of solid, humble status, that'll elevate you and maintain your person.

The risk of it, and damage of man, is when they attain the wealth and recognition to be changed for the prime- negative, when it's personality and character that are the biggest to boost you.

Personality and character conservation, position you, causing you to enter into new relationships, even grandstand. Man has to make God the grandest when awakening, more so than first.

The first of all, is to commune with God, but as I have said, this is important to put God grandest, situated before first, this is counted as unto me also.

TESTAMENT

The activities, it determines, based on if I lean on error, or the whole of faith. When I wake, going to do the daily, it's a pendulum, a sway that must be on one end over the other side.

A man of no chosen side is a scattered and uneven man. An uneven man, or woman, will be bought by all that convinces him or her without power.

But aside from this, it is the inspired one who will alter the damaged point, purposing moreover that trajectory towards Zion. Your trek will be an art, whereas all escapades.

I don't say this to put off the reality of what is right, and what is wrong, I'm saying that the course of this reality, will enable you to motion it poetically.

VOCAL ABOUT JESUS

You can keep to your own devices without recognizing the Situation that brought you to where you are. If you can come to visualize, in the celestial zone, God is the One who is "popular." God is the One who is making the imagery projected.

To not make The One the primary in your sphere because of unseen gain, or embarrassment from a band of vapored people, is your choice and yours to manage. But if you are intending to manage your own misinterpretation of what real and blessed acknowledgment is, then you are to some extent strong, yes, strong but not in prowess, nor valor intending to honor.

Exposing the concealed evils, decreeing to adhere to Jesus Christ, and putting Him further than yourself, putting the wonders of this world and the world to the past of you, is not just the voice of mouth, but your method.

It is your course of action in the midst of a crowd, a crowd trapped and voluntarily overriding the topic of worthy comment, desire, and forum.

MIRACLE

It's never the affair of making yourself known but, in the event of speaking unto what is necessary for your conscience, this you have to make known. To go The Narrow and tread, to know you're the arrow, and fly.

God shall continuously be at the bow. He will aim at His adversities, but it is you that has to be an aspirant, placing yourself in Him and His scope.

Bless the God who omits your giants, because He did omit them. The God that will win on your behalf, will win as winning is as Him. I am before my Lord, before Him that aspires to have every man and woman secured from the force of evil.

"God indeed, will cover you, so I declare thee blessed. My right hand to all, my right hand outstretched over all, the blessing will be."

— Eric Michael Weston

COLOSSAL 24:7

I believe every person is counted in this coliseum of a world. In this cage, the service isn't to them that observe *only* and go; the initial Christian combats adversity every day, and that is what the multitudes are not knowing. In the instance they do know the consecutive pressing of our goal, it is projected that God is God, and He will come.

Pour unwanted in the dirt, and attend the soil to bring up what's to be needed; throw out the vanities in your life, and yield to the, manifestation of upward fruition.

Put the adverse off, so it can't do but meet God.

Please God, I am in the survey too. Pleasing God is enabling grand madness to the devil. This is the tactical Christian, to not become afraid of he who cannot protect himself from a spell. This is the power from Above, to make the world amplified, good passion will win health in all avenues of the man, begetting quality of life.

MEDICAMENT

Real therapy, is ready for the multitudes. The trajectory of this whole world is a graphic scene that is crying, crying for healing.

In the instance of restoration, its solution is that the specific antidote penetrates to produce a curative. The highlighted solution is to recognize the only Clinician who will break the diagnosis.

Jesus Christ passes the procedure of remedying, He will break the prognosis to where, if by your management, it won't come back.

The stress needs to be stressed. This world and living has to be viewed in a technique of countering adversity.

HAREDIM

Humanity is in a place where people are in no place to be severely disconnected from things associated with God. To disconnect from The Connect is opening the door to all else contrary to good. Those that disconnect themselves from life and rest, over to other fill-ins, will soon see their decimation closer than necessary.

You go to where security is, to defend yourself and others; you abandon what will secure you, and you position yourself for fatality. This is the analogical imagery.

The one who disconnects from Life, will position himself or herself for death. Therefore, I feel to say that it is the fear of God, that reverence for Him, that will be the foresight and terminal towards leaving this terrain. The fear of God is linked with love for God.

Haredim is Hebrew and it means "ones who fear God."

COLOSSAL 24:7

Those who fear God to the point of cutting themselves off from society's movement and bustle, and motioning to God and inquiring His ordinances forever will be rewarded, not in monetary unit, not diamond, not gold, but in everlasting immortality.

This is the entire reason why in Christianity, all have to attend the temple of God, the reason why we have to ask for forgiveness frequently, the reason why we in the fold ought to disconnect from what will disconnect us from God.

This is not feasible as making utterance of it; I, too, have to push over the mount called life, the activities of this world, and myself. I have to do what I don't want to do, to be where I'd long to be. I have to not do what I desire to do, so I'm not in a condition I don't want to be in.

To be Christian isn't a casual walk-in to Jesus Christ. You consider Jesus Christ within forever, you now have to toil to the cut forever, or when He calls you to His side, when that time and event will come in for the ones who feared and for the ones who

COLOSSAL 24:7

---

didn't fear. To triumph is to abandon sin.

Goals are met by them that abandon the fanfare and things of little worthiness. It is the person that fears and loves God, trying and doing, proving to all the subject from The Lord, the power from He who blesses and omits from Word.

THEM THAT PRAY

To the one who contains what's "must" inside to endure the lot, when this train is complete, the crown is the award of his or her lifetime. The path to eternal life, is hurdles. It's important to rehearse hell's hurdles to rehearse heaven's serenity. To he who isnt chosing his or her side, the attendees alongside you aspire heavens's vicinity, as you'd aspire.

Them that pray and fellowship with you, are your people, not in the context of skin identicality, nor on the affair of resonating perspective.

The people in the fold, the ones with the exact motive as you to glory, are your people. Hold to what religion is for and against. In this statement, religion as of Christ's way of it and not the course invented by men only.

This world is pretending that what's of God is sensitive, and the devil is firm in emotion than God; this is the lie from satan. Satan is overly sensitive to all

COLOSSAL 24:7

that is God and holiness.It's why he counterfeits all that God does, due to his uncontrollable sensitivity to existence.

The challenges and horrors in life, are to be brought to subdue. The enemy is to be brought to loss of the whole person. The one who used to comply to him, is full fledged to Jesus. Full fledge aim to the God of life, is the key to the doors of this forever inhabitance. It is the greatest, to flank from the adversary to God, to not recede into another trap.

As for me, I'm forward to this move to longevity.

ACKNOWLEDGMENTS

Psalm 91:9-10, 14-16:

Because thou hast made the Lord, which is my refuge, even the most High, thy habitation; there shall no evil befall thee, neither shall any plague come nigh thy dwelling.

Because he hath set his love upon me, therefore will I deliver him: I will set him on high, because he hath known my name. He shall call upon me, and I will answer him: I will be with him in trouble; I will deliver him, and honour him. With long life will I satisfy him, and show him my salvation.

Psalm 107:17, 19-21:

Fools because of their transgression, and because of their iniquities, are afflicted. Then they cry unto the Lord in their trouble, and he saveth them out of their distresses. He sent his word, and healed them, and delivered them from their destructions. Oh that men would praise the Lord for his goodness, and for his wonderful works to the children of men!

Eric Michael Weston

Psalm 118:17:

I shall not die, but live, and declare the works of the Lord.

Matthew 15:30-31:

And great multitudes came unto him, having with them those that were lame, blind, dumb, maimed, and many others, and cast them down at Jesus' feet; and he healed them: insomuch that the multitude wondered, when they saw the dumb to speak, the maimed to be whole, the lame to walk, and the blind to see: and they glorified the God of Israel.

www.ingramcontent.com/pod-product-compliance
Lightning Source LLC
Chambersburg PA
CBHW071143060526
44107CB00131B/186